Also available in the same acetate series:

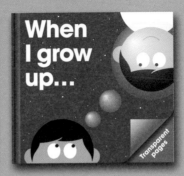

© PatrickGeorge 2016
First published in the United Kingdom in 2012
This revised edition published 2016

www.patrickgeorge.com

ISBN 978-0-9562558-8-4

3 5 7 9 10 8 6 4 2

British Library Cataloguing in Publication Data.
A catalogue record for this book is available from the British Library.

Printed in China.

NUMBERS

Patrick George

10

ten

nine

eight

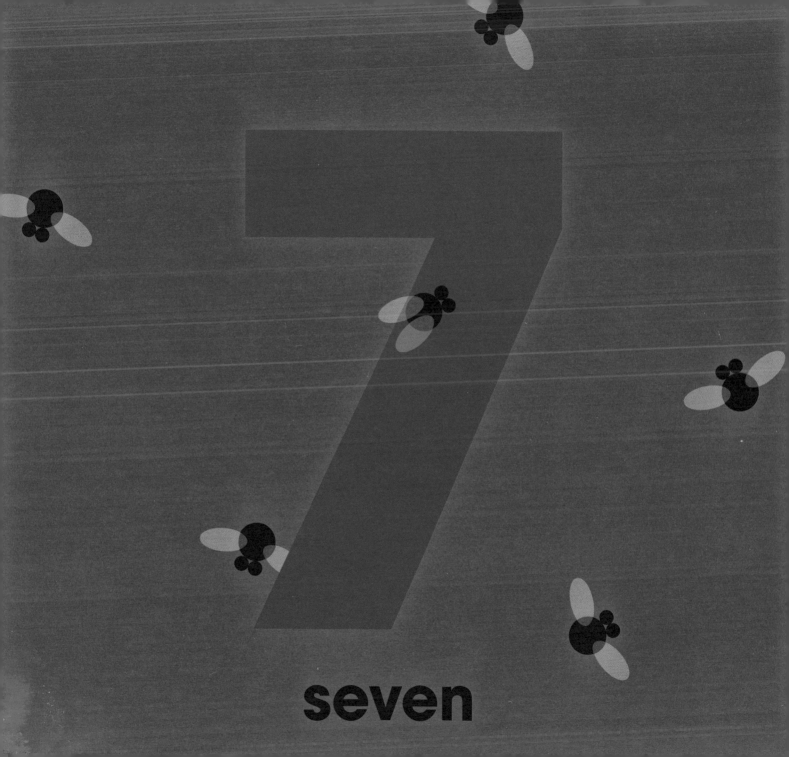

seven

six

five

four

three

2

two

1

one

zero